A Long Walk Home

Dave Eldergill

www.DaveEldergill.org

ISBN: 9781521532447

Dedicated to my Dad

James Walter Eldergill 1934 - 2016

CONTENTS

The beach is a place where a man can feel
He's the only soul in the world that's real
Bell Boy, Quadrophenia,
Pete Townsend 1973

"I expect to be able to see the sea."
"You can see the sea. It's over there between the land and the sky."
Fawlty Towers
John Cleese & Connie Booth 1979

"Man made borders not to limit himself, but to have something to cross."
Anonymous

INTRODUCTION

I am very fortunate. I live in a seaside town and for much of my life I have lived close to the sea, and I too like Mrs Richards from Fawlty Towers, "expect to be able to see the sea". Since the expansion of the railway in Victorian times and the growth of the British seaside holiday resort, there is in our culture an undisputed belief that "to be beside the seaside" is beneficial for one's health, to be able to breath the salubrious sea air and enjoy the restorative benefits of a swim in the ocean is in some way good for you.
We live in an island nation, a visit to the coast from anywhere in this country is always within the possibility of a day trip. But to live in a seaside town is different. It's there all the time and for me it is something very special to have that constant close proximity. Maybe it is in some way comforting having the reassurance of a physical boundary. Knowing there is a definitive edge to my environment, a space between the land and the sky. I also like being used to seeing out to a distant horizon and possibly it is having that as a familiar vista that can act as a counterbalance to the constraints and pressures of modern life. I like to look out and follow the line of the coast to the distance as it confirms my mental construct of where in space I am located. It is a construct that is familiar to me from my lifelong interest in maps. Borders, boundaries and their 2 dimensional cartographic representation have always fascinated me.

As a child I loved to pour over the maps from my dad's National

Geographic magazines, I especially loved seeing the historical changes shown by the fluid fluctuations of national and international borders. This was my first introduction to a new visual language, the 3 dimensional reality represented in a 2 dimensional form with the hint of the exciting potential of something or somewhere new that can be articulated by the border or boundary crossed.

   Whilst these ideas contribute to my preference of residential location, I am sure it must be more than only that. Statistics tell us that nearly half of the worlds population live within 100 kilometres of the coast so I'm not alone in my desire to live where I do. Having always enjoyed walking, I decided I would like to walk the path that follows the coastline around the part of the country I live in. Not just for the obvious health benefits of getting some exercise, but also as an artist, this would be an interesting exploration of my own physical connection with this landscape and my psychological connection with the way I have known the landscape through it's representations. A walking pace allows time for reflection and contemplation and I am hoping that the process of making the journey will in some way help me to gain an understanding of why I feel the need to undertake the journey. As I began to write this journal, I realised that it would not be a descriptive travelogue. This was not going to be a guide to walking the South West Coast Path. There are already many excellent reference books which describe the many varied landscapes of the route around the south west peninsula. I have used some of them myself in planning various stages of the walk. Whilst including some descriptive prose on the wonderful locations I have traveled through, this is less of a comment on what I had seen and more of a consideration and meditation on what I had thought. A useful starting point for making art

CHAPTER 2

DORSET

February 2014
Day 1

The winter storms in January and February 2014 were considered to be be the worst in over 20 years. Strong winds, huge waves and major flooding problems, especially in the South West, made for major transport disruption and unprecedented conditions. It was on one such windy, rainy winter's day that I began the long walk home. A roughly 700 mile walk from the start of the South West Coast Path at South Haven Point, near Poole in Dorset past the official coast path finish in Minehead and on to my home in Burnham on Sea in Somerset.

Over the next 3 years, with day trips and short stays away, the plan was to walk the whole of the coast path in about 50 separate day walks, mostly walking alone, but occasionally sharing the experience with friends. My wife Sharon shared and facilitated the experience, taking the car after each day's start, and being at a prearranged pick up point after the day's walk. How lucky am I. No need to plan my journeys around bus and train timetables.

We began with a difficult car journey across Somerset and Dorset, Sharon , myself and our dear friend Helen who was to accompany me on the first 2 sections. Lashing rain, gale force winds and many flooded roads made for a long trip to the start point and me questioning the wisdom of starting the endeavour on such a day.

We eventually made it to the road that borders Studland Beach and leads to the ferry over to Poole. Once we had pulled into the car park, Helen and I rushed over to a convenient bus shelter to change into walking boots and appropriate clothing. I say appropriate clothing, and obviously I believed myself to be well prepared with good walking socks and boots. Helen, also sensibly had waterproof trousers and raincoat, I on the other hand only had my cotton rain jacket and this proved to be utterly insufficient for the journey ahead. First lesson learned, Equip oneself with suitable clothing for whatever the weather may decide to throw at you!

Sharon left after we had agreed a time and place to rendezvous and we began the days walk to Worth Matravers over 15 miles and 6 hours ahead of us. With heads down and buffeted by the extreme elements, we didn't even see the official marker for the start of the South West Coast Path as we headed off into the unknown.

Not withstanding the weather, this was a good day's hike, along a deserted naturist beach that even the most hardy and dedicated nudists would not brave and through puddles that were deep enough to swim. We even had time for a refreshing cup of tea in a seafront cafe in Swanage.

The short winters day was barely sufficient for the 15 miles we needed to cover and I was concerned because the light was failing by mid afternoon. Our pace increased through the encroaching dark, and we just made it to the warmth of the Square & Compass in Worth Matravers whilst we could still see where we were going

A nice cold pint of local cider seemed to magically ease the tired and aching feet and then our ever reliable lift took us to the Black Bear, a few miles away in Wareham. As the wet clothes and boots dried on the radiators we all enjoyed a good meal and a good nights sleep, ready for the next days walk.

February 2014
Day 2

The sun was out as we left the Black Bear to drive to the start of day 2 of the long walk home. Thoroughly rested and with boots that were only slightly damp, we were ready for what all the guide books I had consulted, described as a "challenging walk" to Lulworth Cove. The coast-path goes steeply up and down with very few level sections, and it took more than 5 hours to walk just over 12 miles. Having previously checked they were open, we passed through the army ranges looking down on the abandoned village of Tyneham and we were careful not to stray off the path, as the signs warning of "military debris" exploding and killing you were slightly disconcerting.

There were not too many other people out walking on the high Dorset cliff paths, cold winds and short days keep most people at home. We did however meet a few other hardy souls. If nature calls when away from civilisation and no facilities are available, then needs be as needs must. We came around a corner as we approached Worbarrow Bay, and saw someone ahead standing next to a rocky outcrop. He said nothing as we got near, and then, whilst passing him, a very embarrassed lady scrambled to her feet, pulling up items of clothing, having been caught in flagrante whilst needing to relieve herself. I can only imagine the severe reprimand her ineffective lookout received once we were out of earshot.

As we neared the end of the day's walk and came down to Lulworth Cove, the heavens opened again. A thunderous downpour soaked me to the skin, after what had been up until then, a cold but clear day. Mental note to self, get a good waterproof for the next time.

So this is it, I am out on the coast path and walking home. The magnificent sweep of the coastline, rising up and down, the white chalk cliffs edged against green fields and heading off into the distant west, make a truly awesome sight. I know this is going to be my magnificent cathedral space where my spirit can soar. This was the line, the boundary, the physical manifestation of the psychological border and I began to get a sense of what doing this walk was actually about.

The journey has begun.

March 2014
Day 3

Arrived at Lulworth Cove by about 10 in the morning, I put on my boots and new raincoat under a grey sky and spitting rain. I was now ready and prepared for the inclement weather to do it's worse, but it soon cleared and I walked mostly in lovely early spring sunshine. I arranged to meet Sharon at the Ferrybridge Inn car park , the other side of Weymouth and allowed my self 6 hours to walk. As I began up the incline away from Lulworth, there were many people out walking. This is a much visited section with the magnificent views down to the arch of Durdle Dor. Soon the crowds thinned out and eventually it seemed I was on my own, just the stunning Dorset scenery for company. I like walking with friends, sharing the experience, but I also love being alone and often as I walk, it is just me. Walking by myself gives me time to think, time to reflect and sometimes time just to be in the moment and concentrate on reaching the next cliff top after the steep climb.

After the very wet weather of the preceding winter, the coast path was extremely muddy in places and thoughts of trying to edge round some of the deep and boggy sludge were soon forgotten. I was glad my boots were waterproof.

I reached Bowleze Cove, and I went down onto the beach. The water was a beautiful blue with white foam crashing against the pebbles and it was refreshing to rest awhile listening to the comforting sound of the sea meeting the land with it's age old, regular rhythm. You can walk all the way along the shore line into

Weymouth but I chose to walk along the path as it is much easier to get purchase on solid ground.

Reaching the town I slowed down and ambled through the familiar vista of The Esplanade, and over the town bridge. Weymouth is a place I know well as we have visited many times. Sharon was born here and we have had numerous holidays in this area with our children. Over the years we have come back again and again, meeting up with Sharon's late father, or going to see her Grandparents. I walk right through the town busy with school children on their way home and eventually reach the car park at Ferrybridge. It wasn't long before he died, that we met up with Clive, Sharon's Dad in the pub there, (with Clive it was always a pub). Now he has gone, it is only fond memories of those encounters that remain , my youthful and protective intolerance long forgotten. Being here again made me realise, how much the South West coast path passed through my history, the places I already knew and remembered. This was going to be more than a physical journey through geographical locations, but also a temporal journey through the landscape of memory, reminding me of the people and places I have known and encountered.

May 2014
Day 4

It was a dull, cloudy day in May when I tackled the next section of the South West Coast Path, the Portland loop. This is the only section where after a days walking I ended up right back where I started.

The weather so often affects perceptions of place and on this grey day Portland seemed to me, an oppressive and unwelcoming Island, tied to Weymouth but very distinct from it. I couldn't put my finger on exactly why. It has so much potential, a seaside location with glorious views over to Weymouth, along the length of Chesil Beach or out into the wide blue of the English channel. And yet the gloominess is palpable and I'm in no hurry to re-visit.

After parking the car in the Ferrybridge Inn car park I began walking along Chesil Bank. A carpet of spring flowers was bursting from beneath the pebbled ridge, and I attempted to take a photograph as I didn't know what they were and wanted look them up later. The leadened sky seemed to mute their potential glory and I realised I wasn't witnessing them at their best. Unfortunately trying to walk over the loose pebbles was very hard and it was difficult to make progress as the shingle shifted under the weight of each step. After 10 minutes of slow laborious movement I realised I would need to head down to the firmer ground of the tarmac pavement so I ended up crossing the isthmus by walking alongside the road. With cars hurtling by, it made for an unpleasant trek over to Portland and it was perhaps this that coloured my first impression of the area.

I choose to keep the sea to my left, as with the rest of my journey and therefor walked around the island in a clockwise direction. My 14 mile route took me up through a housing estate, passed the razor wired fence of the young offenders institution and out to the Portland Bill lighthouse. I then turned and followed the west side of the island, past more grim looking housing, through the quarries of Portland stone and down through Fortuneswell before retracing my steps back along the road to Ferrybridge. Why did an area of obvious natural beauty feel like the worst sink estate in the west? Was it the battleship grey of the ubiquitous stone reflecting the overcast sky? Was it the naval past or the long history as a place of imprisonment that imbued the atmosphere with dark forebodings or was it just me? Ether way, I felt relieved when I was back in the car and driving home.

May 2014
Day 5

2 weeks later and I'm back at the Ferrybridge inn car park again. The sun is shining and it feels warm on my face. Today is going to be a long walk of over 18 miles to the Hive Beach cafe near Burton Bradstock but it will mostly be on the level and the weather is fantastic.

The 11 miles to Abbotsbury follow the Fleet, the lagoon separated from the sea by the shingle bank which is Chesil Beach. I go past fields of yellow rapeseed vivid against the blue sky and it feels all is well with the world.

We stayed at the Bagwell Farm campsite which is near here, with our close friends Rob and Sal a few years ago, and I remembered walking down across fields then, and thinking how beautiful the countryside in this area truly is. The path leads away from the Fleet and up on to the hill with majestic views down across Chesil and out to sea. I walk past the golden stone of St Catherine's chapel, a beacon on the hill I have so often seen before whilst driving along the coast road to Weymouth. The route crosses lush green fields and eventually makes its' way back down to the beach for the last miles to the cafe and a reviving cup of tea.

I have been writing a song using a particular guitar riff I had been working on, just like I did when I played in a band as a teenager. So much of the music I listened to in the 1970s was based on the short rhythmic musical phrases played by my guitar heroes of the time. It was with this in mind, that as I walked I began to put together the lyrics for the song "77"

We grew our hair
Played a mean guitar in the air
Put on the Floyd
Turned up the volume till Dad got annoyed
Ziggy stardust rocked
Saw him on Top of the Pops
Crazy paint, and gold flared jeans

It got too big
Under the shadow of a flying pig
So you cut your hair
Like Joey Ramone, you don't care...
You said John Peel was best
And the old grey whistle test

Everything had to be, brand new

**God saved the queen
Rotten Johnny spat it out obscene
And Ian Durey told
Of sex and drugs and rock and roll
At a street party
For the silver jubilee
You pushed a pin through your nose**

**We formed had a band
Got an old guitar in my hand
Only knew three chords
Nobody needed any more
We thought we were great
But the drummer would come in late
It didn't matter at that time
At that time.**

May 2014
Day 6

We stayed last night in Weymouth and I was grateful not to have to drive back to Somerset after yesterday's long walk. Today's journey has taken me the 13 or so miles into Lyme Regis. It included an unfortunate detour away from the coast at Charmouth as land slips had made parts of the coast path unsafe but it did mean I was able to call in at a grocer's shop and replenish my dwindling supply of fluids. I went through the little coastal towns of West Bay and Seatown, mingling with holiday makers before passing them by and heading back onto the coast path. Sitting on a bench by the little harbour at West Bay, I ate an ice cream but felt a disconnect with the smiling faces all around me. They were visiting and had arrived at their destination, I was just passing through.

  This magnificent stretch of coastline includes Golden Cap. It is the highest point on the South coast and with the clear and sunny conditions today I was able see all the way back to Portland and ahead as far as Start Point. Looking back at the miles already covered and forward to the path stretching ahead, the scale of the task and my own insignificance against this ancient landscape was a little humbling

The creative process for me is built on hours of seemingly unproductive time, when thoughts and ideas swirl around without finding concrete conclusions. Today the space and slow continuous progress of my walking gave me opportunity to reflect on the DRI art project research. I had recently visited Joan Chester, a nurse who trained in Derby in the 1940's. We had talked about nursing and her vastly different and yet similar journey to mine. As a visual artist I strive to find ways to visually articulate these thoughts and experiences. Joan had shown me her note book, a list written in a beautiful hand script detailing the instrument requirements of different surgeons and the various operations they performed. Such a powerful historical document and also a visual communication of something more profound. I will somehow make work which includes this!

May 2014
Day 7

I am joined today by my friend Rob for the section from Lyme Regis to Seaton. Today's walk will go slightly inland and away from the coast and this is a little disappointing. The famous undercliffs route has been closed due to landslips and the coast path leading away from Lyme Regis follows a diversion. I am however, walking a boundary and the nature of boundaries is they are not fixed or stable but change over time. Whether that's the political changes as empires come and empires fall, or the slower but equally inescapable changes as the forces of nature erode and sculpt an ever changing landscape.

We also cross a border. Dorset is left behind and the coast of south Devon awaits. This is my first transition from one county to another, a mere change of name, a faint line on my ordnance survey map, a human construct which makes no difference to my progress and yet I am excited by the prospect. It is an excitement which goes way back into my youth. As a child, when driving with my family to stay in Germany, I can vividly remember my anticipation of crossing out of France and into Belgium. It was as if this political line on a map, which even then did not require passport control or customs searches, was indicative of something more profound than simply moving physically forward, from one nation state to an other. I'm sure over the course of my long walk home these are notions and ideas that will occupy much of my thinking.

Rob and I walk along the beach front in Lyme, passed the excited laughter of children paddling in the still cold water, and up through dense woodland away from the coast. Rhododendrons are in full bloom and although the day is overcast there is a sense of Spring giving way to Summer.

We walk around 8 miles and barely get a glimpse of the sea. The East Devon countryside breaking out in anticipation of the coming warmth and longer days. It's not long before we come down across a golf course with a view of Seaton and the coast ahead. Following a steep descent we are back on the sea front of a seaside town, another stage of the adventure completed.

CHAPTER 2

SOUTH DEVON

June 2014
Day 8

I needed to wear a sunhat today! I was walking for over 6 hours and there was only an occasional wispy cloud in the blue, blue sky. I began with a nice stroll along the Esplanade in Seaton. It is still early and there aren't too many people about. Passing the colourful beach huts I prepare for the first of today's many climbs. The view back over the town and out to the hazy hulk of Portland in the far distance is worth the effort.

Down from the sandstone cliffs and entering Sidmouth, I find a busy seafront in full holiday mode, the tempting smell of chips reminding me that I was hungry and ready for a lunch break. My inclination is to wait untill I have passed through and am back on a less busy stretch of coast, all these people are a distraction from my thoughts.

The ongoing art project based around the Derbyshire Royal Infirmary occupies much of my thinking. I have been watching the BBC tv series from the early 1990's called *Cardiac Arrest*. It is written from a junior doctors perspective, and not very sympathetic to nurses but manages to capture some of reality of working in a NHS hospital back when I was training as a nurse. Revisiting this program was a nostalgic reminder of that time, and was a powerful contrast to the strange and mournful experience I had earlier this year when I walked round the abandoned and derelict remains of the old hospital. At times like these when I am walking, I very rarely get a finished piece of work in my mind, but I have the time to mull over ideas and feelings which will often kick start something more concrete at a later date. The memory of that visit to Derby, is very much in my mind and I know that this will be the focus of a whole body of work, still to come.

Ahead I see a white chalk cliff face giving way to the rust red Devon sandstone, which bleeds a dark stain into the sea at the bottom of the precipice. I pass the Landram Bay holiday park which is separated from the edge of the cliff by the coast path and I find myself thinking about of one of our first times in a caravan with our children when they were very young, and we stayed at this site. It was a tiny little van and yet we all fitted in. I have an unfortunate ear worm of the children's song called *Ollie the Otter* going around my head. Funny thing memory, this silly children's verse, from a long ago holiday now playing like a stuck record in my mind.

After more than 16 long and strenuous miles I am approaching today's finish at Budleigh Salterton and see the pebble beach up ahead. But I have made a slight miscalculation, I am very tired but unfortunately had forgotten that to reach the town I must walk inland by the river Otter, over a footbridge and back down the other side adding more than a mile extra to the end of the day's journey, oh well I will sleep like a log tonight!

July 2014
Day 9

I'm sat in a little cafe in Exmouth, waiting for the ferry to take me across the estuary of the River Exe to Starcross. It's been a nice steady 6 miles from Budleigh Salterton and I have half an hour before the ferry leaves. Sipping my hot cup of sweet tea, I'm occupied by the way my physical journey is weaving through the many, many memories located in this landscape, and I am now of an age where there are many, many memories. Childhood days on the beach at Exmouth with my cousins. A week spent in my parents timeshare hotel room in a sea front hotel, they had satellite television and we watched an episode of Star Trek Deep Space Nine, such a novelty at the time! A holiday trip along the river, with our friends Andy and Shirley and all the children. It is strange and difficult to understand the way relationships can change over time. Sometimes interests and passions develop and grow along parallel lines and sometimes those lines diverge and the nature of relationships can also move apart. Often there is no rhyme and reason, it is just the way of the journey.

Deep in thought I nearly miss the boat. It takes about 15 minutes to slowly chug across the mouth of the river. Rivers so often constitute a border, a natural blue line on a map. But on this coastal walk, this river is another physical boundary to cross, a deep indentation into the edge of the land before continuing on the other side.

I go past the gaudy seaside amusements at Dawlish Warren and again it is the childhood memories that come flooding back. The school holidays were one long endless warm sunny day after another, it never rained and every moment was the blissful fun of carefree youth, at least that's how I remember them. Leaving Dawlish and the selective memories behind I walk down by the sea wall alongside Brunel's magnificent coastal railway into Teignmouth, only recently reopened following the storm damage earlier in the year.

The day ends with another boat trip. The River Teign can be

crossed over by a road bridge to Shaldon but the little foot passenger ferry is running and I feel it very fitting to cross this border sat in the small boat, down close to the water. It was a nice way to finish the day's journey.

July 2014
Day 10

We are staying for a week at our caravan in Devon. Helen is with us and she is recovering from a minor operation. I have two days along the coast path planned, and in her state of recuperation she has decided to join me for the last section of the first day and the beginning of the next. I'm dropped at Shaldon and arrange to meet the girls about 4 hours later for a late lunch in Torquay. Many times I have walked this section of the coast path and I know all the steep ascents and descents to come. I don't feel I can miss this part out, just because I have already been along this route. This walk is about following a continuous line, albeit not in one complete go. For that line to be continuous it is a necessity to begin each new day's journey at the point were the previous walk ended. It marks the boundary and has a continuity of purpose. The route of the coast path sometimes will hug the edge of the land and follow an estuary inland until the first bridge is reached, at other points such as my last walk, the path crosses the blue boundary using an existing ferry service. My one concession to the rule of the continuous line, is allowing one days walk to finish at the ferry point and when necessary starting the next day's journey from the other side, the only parts that I may miss out are those where the route would allow me to sit down and let a boat do the traveling for me.

 The 11 miles into Torquay traverse green fields with docile cows, through woodlands, alongside beaches and through familiar townscapes, the red Devon earth under my feet. As a child much of my growing up was away from the family home in Devon. We lived in various locations abroad when my dad was in the army and up in Essex when my dad first qualified as a teacher. Torquay was always our root, the family's grounding and we would return between army postings, whilst Dad trained as a teacher and for nearly every summer holiday when we lived away. It was seeing the colour of the Devon soil that was the first marker, the first signifier that we were home. Wherever we were living, we knew we were back in Devon by the red of the land.

There is a steep climb up from Oddicombe beach and under the funicular railway and on towards Babbacome. This is the part of Torquay where my mum grew up, and I know this area well, from my own experiences and from seeing the precious memories taken by my grandad with his 9.5mm film cine camera.

I have some of that old film footage, my mother and her siblings on the beach at Oddicombe. Transferred to digital, I can watch it on the computer screen. The faded black and white images have a ghostly presence as a white shape caused by the centre sprocket holes, rises through the film. An uninvited ethereal entity trying to escape from the captured moment in time, reliving again and again that family day out on the beach.

My grandad loved new technology, and was an avid maker of home movies in the 1930s. And when, as a child I visited with my brothers, sisters and cousins, we would sit on the floor in their home in Torquay, and he would show us old black and white films on his home projector. The clickety click of the sprockets the only sound to accompany our laughter at the antics of "Our Gang" in a 1920's short film by Hal Roach called "No Noise" or our childhood terror at the "creature from the black lagoon"

After a nice lunch and refreshing cold drink in town, Helen and I walk along Torquay seafront, passed Corbyn Head and Livermead, the coast path taking us on the main road for part of the journey. We could easily be in the South of France and on this sunny warm July day I can see why they call this the English Riviera. As we come into

Paington, children are diving into the turquoise sea which doesn't look as cold as my common sense tells me it must be, even though it is a warm summer's afternoon. We stop at the beach at Goodrington and telephone Sharon who is coming to pick us up. It will be a little while until she gets here, so the boots are off, sheer joy for the tired aching feet. The sands are crowded with holiday makers and there are many people having fun splashing about in the shallow surf. I am hot after the long walk and although I know that the cold water will be a shock to the system, the temptation is too much. I can't resist and down to my shorts I am also in the sea for a reviving swim.

July 2014
Day 11

Sharon dropped Helen and I back at Goodrington around eleven, and we walked around the Torbay coast path into Brixham. I have often taken the Ferry boat across from Torquay harbour so it was nice to see this coastline close up and from the land side. It is a coastline of beautiful little coves and secluded beaches before it enters the fishing port of Brixham. Helen and I chat as we walk and I really appreciate that there are parts of this journey when I am not walking alone. I replenish my water and leave Helen and Sharon to explore the Brixham charity shops whilst I carry on around Berry Head and on to Dartmouth.

When walking, thoughts can seem random and obscure, the obvious contemplation of the magnificent scenery, the practical considerations of where to put my feet and decisions about when I should put on my sun hat, due to today's powerful rays.

I was also thinking about our move to Burnham. The view from our flat, over the beach and out towards the headlands in Devon , Somerset and Wales has had an effect on my relationship to the coast. Living on the seafront draws the feelings I have about being in a coastal place into sharper focus. If the tide is in or way out as it can be along the Bristol Channel, if the air is clear and the visibility like crystal, or if the haze obscures the view, the sea is always there and it is a constant presence. This ongoing relationship with the sea is in part the reason for undertaking this long walk home. Living here also has an impact on my creativity. Burnham is a creative place, a magnet for artists and musicians, its' atmosphere feeding into my art. I hadn't spent much time playing my guitar over the last 20 years but now I am finding melodies and lyrics are filling my mind and new songs are being written. It isn't a case of sitting down and thinking, "what shall I write about?" But rather as I'm out walking, letting the thoughts and issues that surround me find their natural expression. The news is full of the terrible situation in Syria and Iraq. Why is the world so full of pain and suffering? Why are people so full of hate that their selfish desires give way to evil deeds? Yet in the midst of all the horror, there are those who forget about self, put their own lives in danger and go out and help. Sharon has a book by Rob Bell called "Love Wins". I haven't read it but the title struck a chord. I do believe that good is stronger than evil. In spite of the media's insistence in only reflecting the worst of humanity, there is a power in the universe, a gravitational attraction which ultimately wins!

Love wins, love always wins
Sometimes it seems the fight
Is lost to this cruel world
Where might is deemed to be right
Conquer the night with love
And don't loose sight of love
I'll always try to love
Cos love wins

Love wins, love always wins
The wisdom of my youth
Through all the pain I've seen
Can I believe that truth
So I hold on to love
And don't despair of love
The greatest of these is love
Cos love wins

Love wins, love always wins
So many times I fail
If I, have not love
My voice a clanging bell
And I forgive through love
And turn from hate through love
The only way is love
Cos love wins

Today is the hottest of the year so far. The heat haze shimmering over dry fields and cracked earth as the path, far away from the nearest road, winds down to near empty beaches. The trail takes me right down to the beach at Scabbacombe Sands, the water blue and inviting. It would be nice to stop and take a short break at this idyllic location. There are very few people about, as this is a fair walk from the nearest car park. I decide I'll just take off my boots and paddle so sit down on the sand. It is only then that I notice that the few people who are here are enjoying the full benefit of the sun unencumbered by clothing. Well that water does seem very appealing in the 30 degree heat, so I too am tempted to swim and when in Rome…

   It's still quite a few miles until I reach the ferry at Kingswear and cross over the Dart to meet with my lift back. There are some difficult climbs and descents and the heat takes its toll. I have seriously underestimated just how much fluid is needed to stay hydrated and as my supply is extinguished I begin to experience thirst like I've never experienced before. I pass the coast watch station at Forward Point and consume the bottle of water the volunteer gives me with sheer delight. Only 2 or so miles now, down through cooler woodland to reach the ferry.

   On the other bank, I see Sharon and Helen waving, as the boat is slowly pulled through the water. My head feels as though I have a hangover, I'm nauseous and tired. Sharon has got life saving orange juice and water waiting for me as the ferry pulls in. No matter what the weight, from now on I will always carry enough fluids.

July 2014
Day 12

It is another lovely sunny day, and although the route will take me
past a few places where I can replenish my supplies I will be taking
no chances and I am carrying plenty of drinks. Sharon drops me on
the quayside and I walk up the slight incline towards Dartmouth
Castle. I love this feeling at the start of the day's walk. I'm full of
energy and eager anticipation of what the day's journey will bring.
There is a spring in my step and a lightness to my movement. The
tired, aching walker who reached Dartmouth 3 weeks ago is just a
distant memory . The views over the river, with the sail boats and
pleasure yachts, are a watercolour painters dream, and I stop to take
in this English summer idyl. I go on through woodland and sheltered
coves before the path rounds the headland and away from the river. I
know this area, from many holidays and from visits to my parents
when they lived in the nearby village of Strete. I have sunbathed and
swam at these beaches, I have driven along this coast road, eaten in
local pubs and restaurants. I have been to the local church where my
father was pastor and met the local people who are still here after all
the summer visitors have gone. But now I am walking its' perimeter,
following the edge of the land and getting a new perspective, gaining
an unfamiliar look at the familiar and this is part of what makes the
"long walk home" the rewarding experience it is.

 Passing by the picture postcard beach of Blackpool Sands, I walk
through fields owned and farmed by one of my father's former
congregation. I have tasted the succulent roast beef, fed and reared
on this land and I can vouch for its outstanding quality.

 It does seem strange to walk through the village of Strete before
heading back down to the beach at Strete gate, and not be able to
visit my parents for a cup of tea. They had only recently moved back
to be nearer to the family in Somerset. Their journey now passing

into the homeward stretch and as life moves on and so must I.

Sharon is waiting at the carpark halfway along Slapton Sands and we eat ice creams before I head off towards Torcross and the memorial to the American troops who lost their lives here during the preparations for the D~Day landings in 1945.

That a peaceful holiday location was the site of such tragedy is difficult to imagine. I wonder if the landscape retains anything of the memory of the events that scar it or does it heal and leave no trace? A few years ago when visiting the memorial at Vimy Ridge, site of a major First World War battle, I was taken aback by how peaceful it seemed. Lush and abundant woodland areas were roped off due to the sheer amount of unexploded ordinance, the trees reclaiming and healing the once scared earth. The fears and horrors were no longer tangible in the air. Is it time that slowly takes away the vestiges of evil, perhaps it is that nature will not be subdued by mankind's toxic influence. I don't know the answer. I have been to buildings that still hold something of a grim past in their very fabric. I think of the old workhouse in Southwell, Nottinghamshire. The sadness ingrained into the walls. Maybe it is because it is a man made structure that it still waits for nature to redeem.
I end the day at the lighthouse at Start Point having passed by what is left of Hallsands, lost to the power of the sea and the dredging of shingle for building of the naval dockyard near Plymouth. Looking out across the hazy blue of Lyme bay I can just make out Portland, over 100 miles of walking behind me.

August 2014
Day 13

As this journey has progressed, I have had the relevant ordnance survey explorer map with me. The metric 4 cm to each kilometre scale ideal for my slowly deteriorating middle aged eyesight to follow. I will pre-plan each day, read up on the next section I am about to walk and work out where it will be convenient for picking up and setting down. This is information readily available on the web and with informative web sites, google maps and street view, easy to do from the comfort of my armchair, iPad in hand. There is however something about the 2 dimensional representation of the 3 dimensional reality in the os map that seems easy for me to understand. Spread out on the floor, following the line on the map I can visualise in my mind how the landscape will be. I have grown up reading this language and feel comfortable with the familiar pictorial representations.

The coast path is not really a navigational challenge, the sea is on the left, the land to the right and the way ahead, usually well signposted with the acorn symbol, is easy to see. Occasionally the official path moves far enough inland to lose sight of the water and sometimes there are necessary diversions due to land slips. The old faithful ordnance survey provides the reassurance that I am located exactly where I'm supposed to be, with national grid references placed on convenient posts all along the coast path. Today that is on a wonderful and almost deserted stretch of coast from the lighthouse at Start Point, around the most southernmost part of Devon, Prawle Point and on to Salcombe. The wooden coast path sign tells me I have 462 miles to go to Minehead, and I have already travelled at least 168 miles so far.

This is rugged and challenging coastal walking. A narrow path which in places teeters on the edge of some steep drops, and I am grateful for the dry conditions, this would be much more difficult on a wet, muddy and slippery path. I don't see a soul until I'm heading back up the next estuary towards East Portlemouth and the little passenger ferry over to meet Sharon. I really enjoy the variety of the coast, small little coves or long unspoilt beaches, fishing ports or coastal towns but today's journey feels like I'm hugging the edge of the land, right on the boundary of earth, sea and sky.

September 2014
Day 14

Mid September and I am fortunate to be favoured with glorious late summer sunshine, I leave the river estuary, past the little beach of South Sands and along through pleasant woodland and back onto more rugged coastline. I will end today at Bantham beach and not take the ferry over the river Avon towards Bigbury, but will start my next walk on the other side. This is truly beautiful scenery and even after this year's warm summer the grass is still a lush green. There are other walkers about and also people out "ruining a good walk" as I pass by the golf course. There are plenty of holidaymakers in Hope Cove, those for whom this last vestige of summer is the tonic to endure the coming shorter days. This part of South Devon has been one of our favourite holiday destinations over the years and being here again naturally triggers memories. I can't now imagine spending a whole day on the beach, but when the children were younger we came here as a large group of friends. We swam, sunbathed, ate sandwiches crunchy with sand and watched our friend Rob not giving the children an inch as he determined to win at beach cricket. Four families all agreeing on how to spend a day of our joint holiday. Children of similar ages are a connection, part of the glue that cements friendships together and it is only natural that as children grow some of those connections can also begin to unravel. But being here again now, reminds me that the passage of time not only adds to life's rich tapestry but also looses and unties some of those threads and todays lovely walk is tinged with a degree of sadness.

September 2014
Day 15

Walking again today with Helen and it's another lovely September day of blue sky and warm sun. We are on a deadline. Four miles on from Bigbury we will reach the estuary of the River Erme. The river can be waded across an hour either side of low tide but any later and it would mean a seven mile detour inland. I believed we had plenty of time but it's quite a steep incline up from Bigbury and our progress was slower than I anticipated. Reaching the river, well over an hour later, we meet a couple, with boots hanging from their necks and walking poles in each hand. They had just crossed over from the other side. They were seasoned hikers and must have been in their eighties and if they could cross then so could we. Rolling up our trousers we began the crossing but realised we were behind schedule and the water would be over our knees. Todays walk was over 13 miles and I wasn't keen to add the extra 7 so there was no time to lose. Trousers off, we waded up to our thighs in the clear, cold water and were soon drying off sitting on the sandy beach opposite.

This is an undeveloped, remote and stunningly beautiful part of the Devon coast and as we came around Gara Point, we caught sight in the slowly turning to grey distance, the first glimpse of the next county. Ahead to the West was Cornwall. I must be getting used to walking this path and the ups and downs on this section were less tiring for me than for Helen but I unfortunately underestimated how long it would take us to reach our rendezvous at the pub in Noss Mayo. A poor phone signal didn't help with the need to communicate our slower than expected pace with Sharon and there was some confusion with meeting up. But, all's well that ends well and we did get our lift back.

October 2014
Day 16

It's a grey, overcast day when I start again, on the west side of the river Yealm at Warren Point and a month since I finished at Noss Mayo on the East side. Since then I have been back to Derby and revisited the sight of the old hospital again. I also attended a meeting of the Derby Nurses League and chatted with some of the ex-nurses, reminiscing about their experiences of the Infirmary. I'm grateful to have this opportunity, alone with my thoughts. I need to let my recent experiences ruminate in my mind, and as fall of my feet and sound of my breathing move me onward, ideas begin to form. I have begun to make some sketches, mixing with images of the 1940's nurses notebook and new work is beginning to emerge.

I go around Wembury bay and up into Plymouth Sound and against the occasional light shower of rain, I pull tight the hood of my raincoat and deeper into thought.

The path takes on a new character and gives way to the urban sprawl of the largest mass of humanity on the South West coast. It seems strange to be following the little acorn signs past houses, and along a stretch of main road, across Laira bridge and into an industrial estate. I have walked the edge of every coastal town so far but Plymouth is on a different scale altogether, more than eight miles of walking, away from the familiar green with hard unyielding tarmac under foot. The diversity of the coast is fascinating, at one point I'm in a wild desolate landscape, tasting the salt air and watching the untamed power of the sea and later the same day I'm getting out of the way as a smelly diesel lorry reverses into a business park. I finish the day's walk by the landing jetty for the Cremyll ferry, right next to a pub called "The Vine," a sign in the window declaring it to be the last pub in Devon. I now have nearly 300 miles of Cornish coastline to walk before I'm back on the Devon path.

CHAPTER 3

SOUTH CORNWALL

November 2014
Day 17

November and the days are getting short so this will be my last coastal walk this year. Today I am going to cross the river Tamar, the border between Devon and Cornwall, or as some see it, the border between England and Cornwall. Whenever I've been here before, there has always been the sense of entering somewhere different. I don't know if this is because the pre-Saxon Celtic identity and language remained, along with the Welsh, Scots and Irish, long after the rest of post-Roman Britain morphed into England. Also it could be effected because of geography. It is a peninsula jutting out into, and surrounded on three sides, by the sea. The River Tamar almost creates an island. Cornwall is not passed through on the way to anywhere else, it is the end destination. As someone who has lived in a tourist location, I know the begrudging acceptance of the hordes of summer visitors. Tolerated as essential for the local economy but seen so often as "other" and in Cornwall, I have always felt I am "other". One of the thousands of seasonal "emmets" from "up country" (we knew them as "grockles" when I lived in Torquay). I have no direct bad experience on which to base this feeling and perhaps I'm projecting my own childhood prejudices, but I see the

Welcome to Cornwall sign from the ferry as it pulls into Cremyll, and I know I am across the frontier and in a foreign land.

There are fantastic autumnal colours in the woodlands of the Mount Edgecoombe Estate and the light rain doesn't detract from the natural beauty. I take the occasional photo as I have done throughout this journey and wonder about why as artists we have the need to capture and re- present the sensory delights that nature gives without effort.

I make my way to Portwrinkle along the length of Whitsand bay, through the little coastal villages of Kingsand and Cawsand as the sun emerges and the sky clears. My first taste of walking the Cornish coast is out of season, and there are very few people about. The sleepy acceptance of the coming change to winter evident as I pass empty and closed summer chalets. I too will now wait for the longer days and warming sun before making my way all the way down to the Atlantic fringe that marks the lands end and the sea's dominion.

March 2015
Day 18

It's a new year, the lazy winter in which my greatest desire has been to hibernate, is slowly turning to spring. I have decided to try and walk on 2 or 3 consecutive days now the journey is taking me further and further away from home. A couple of out of season nights in a Cornish premier inn will hopefully enable me to cover quite a few miles walking with each trip away.

I am back in the village of Portwrinkle looking out over a grey and murky Whitsand Bay, ready to begin today's journey to Polperro. The first climb back onto the footpath strains on dormant and out of condition leg muscles. Wet and muddy underfoot, it is difficult to get purchase and progress is quite slow. At one point along the route, a foggy mist rolls in from the sea and the poor visibility even further diminishes my pace.

I may not have walked much over the winter but the Infirmary Project is moving forward. Juxtaposing found audio content from YouTube with edited video from various sources I can see results which tie together so many different threads. Threads which include, a deep historical relationship with a Christian metanarrative within our culture, and a familiarity with its forms and structures. Before beginning the research for this project, I had never read any, of the Book of Common Prayer, but sentences such as "ashes to ashes and dust to dust," "man that is born of a woman" and "dearly beloved we are gathered here to today" have been an integral part of the cultural landscape I inhabit. Through the milestone events in life, such as births marriages and death, which this work is referencing, and through the consumption of film, television and various media these familiar forms of that Christian story constitute something of the fabric of the culture, which informs who I am. I am also aware that I want to connect the work with the tripart stained glass window from the hospital chapel, now housed in St Peter's Church in Derby. The form of triptych is providing a grounding point to the various strands of expression this work is taking and has a rich history within the traditions of religious art. Originally a triptych would have been a devotional art work consisting of three panels, often with the panels being hinged so that the outer sections could be closed over the middle section. It was a very common form of altar piece art from the medieval period onwards, and the form together with the subject matter and content of the painted panels was part of the meaning of the work. It is a form which has moved beyond the traditional altar piece and includes Francis Bacon's *figures at the base of a crucifixion* and Bill Viola's video work the *Nantes Triptych*. My video editing skills have been benefiting from the input of Ignite Somerset and the video pieces I have been working on over the winter are now coming together using this form.

The weather and poor visibility give me plenty of opportunity to reflect on how the project is going and before long I find myself coming down into the small town of Looe. It is surprisingly busy with people, considering the rain, so I make my way over the bridge, along the other side of the water and back out on to pleasingly empty coastal path for a few more miles before ending the day at Polperro.

March 2015
Day 19

It's a brighter day and only a short drive to Polperro, where today's walk begins, from where we stayed last night, so I'm able to fill up on a full English breakfast and still begin the journey relatively early. Polperro is a typical Cornish fishing village with narrow streets and not at all car friendly, so we pull into the car park at the top of the hill and I get on my boots before walking down through the quaint and touristy town to rejoin the coast path. I'm soon up overlooking the estuary and able to see the jagged rocks jutting out into the sea on the headland where I walked yesterday. The view is clear and sharp after yesterday's rain.

This is the coastline of the tourist brochure, crystal clear water reflecting the blue sky. Granite cliffs with swirling white foam where they meet the sea, and empty sandy beaches. I walk the roller coaster route of the path, down into wooded valleys and back up to a green carpet of verdant grass. I take the little ferry across the water at Fowey and then again leave the confines of civilisation and back onto this magnificent coast. Sharon is waiting to meet me at Parr Sands and we take the short drive back to our overnight accommodation. I have covered more than 28 miles in two days and have about 12 to do tomorrow and I feel that after my winter's sojourn I have given myself a good start to this next part of the journey.

March 2015
Day 20

From Parr Sands I walk through what seems to be an abandoned industrial site, part of the china clay industry in this part of Cornwall, along past a golf course and eventually to Carlyon Bay. This was once a thriving holiday complex and I remember bringing the children here years ago. Time has blurred the sharp edges of memory and I struggle to recollect, was it when we were visiting our friends

Michael and Karen when they lived in Bodmin, or was it on holiday with Andy and Shirley? Our friend Rob has a pinpoint accurate recollection of events, he can tell you where, when and with whom. The weather and how Derby County performed on that week also feature in this memory miracle. Often all I get is a vague sense of something not quite known, the linear progress of time has in someway slipped from the rails. It could be a smell that evokes an emotion or an unrelated connection that triggers something else. One aspect still clear from long ago, is remembering seeing dolphins out in the bay from the cliff top path. On this trip, and I have now walked over 270 miles along the edge of the sea, I have not seen a single dolphin.

The holiday complex is no more, derelict buildings and piles of rubble give the impression of a post apocalyptic wasteland. It seems that a former site of merriment and fun is somehow more forlorn and sad when it has been left to decay. It is different from the derelict remains of the DRI, the ghosts of the past there, not quite so tragic and melancholy.

I walk on to finish the day at Mevagissey and go past Porthpean beach. Now this I do remember, an out of season day with Michael and Karen in the 1980s. I can't do the specifics like Rob, the precise year or exact month remain unknown but the location and the name trigger memories and as I walk down onto the beach the sense of being here before, and of having fun times with friends, comes flooding back.

March 2015
Day 21

We have another 2 nights away, so again I'm hoping to walk a good distance before heading back from Cornwall. It took over two and half hours to drive to the start point in Mevagissey and I want to make the most of being so far from home.

We park up by the harbour and I begin walking the road up Polkirt Hill, past the expensive holiday cottages with their wonderful views and up to where the footpath leaves the road to Chapel Point. I'm still needing to wear a fleece and hat as the sunshine struggles against a deceptively cool wind blowing in from the sea. The path has a flow, it meanders along. Sometimes it winds and turns me down to the waves and I can walk the waters edge before it leads me back up to the breathtaking views out to the deep blue. I have to navigate, follow my map, have a schedule to meet Sharon, and this is all part of the walking experience but sometimes that is mentally put to one side. I am in the moment walking in the now and not really thinking of anything but just being. I know I will be in Portloe by about 5pm, I am used to my pace and I have planned the route before I began, so for now, the schedule can be forgotten. There is no one here in this glorious and magnificent open sky cathedral, but me and nature and it feels good.

March 2015
Day 22

Today it is my intention to reach St Anthony on the West side of the river Fal. I am not going to be tied by the ferry timetables for crossing the estuary but will begin tomorrows walk in Falmouth on the other side. We have booked into a small b/b in the town for tonight. Yesterdays sun has gone and the sea is lacklustre and a brooding grey, sending rolling mists back onto the land. I see a large house in the distance, it's lawn sweeping down to the coast path, it seems familiar and as I get nearer I remember it from the TV adaptation of Mary Wesley's novel, "The Camomile Lawn", set during the second world war. I enjoyed that series for many reasons but what sticks in the mind most is seeing the characters running along the coast path near here and thinking then, that there was something magnificent about the location. Something meaningful about the setting on the edge of the world when the real world was also balanced on the edge of the abyss and about to be dramatically turned upside down by the coming war. The desire to undertake this journey is influenced by so many things and perhaps that little gem of

90's television drama has played part in me being here now.

The fog becomes more dense and more persistent, the visibility diminishes and my perspective has to change. Gone is my contemplation of the wide open view, all there is now is my immediate vicinity. Every step is carefully trod as I can no longer see further than a few meters in front. This is quite scary walking, the cliff edge and drop down in an unforgiving sea never that far. From the old fort at St Anthony I walk along a comforting stretch of tarmac road with only safe fields on each side, to meet up with Sharon. She too has struggled to find our meeting up point, the poor visibility stretching further and further inland. I'm glad to reach our overnight stop and put my boots and coat out to dry, thankful the only water that surrounds me now is coming from the head of a warming and reviving shower.

March 2015
Day 23

It's raining and blowing a gusty wind as I leave the guest house in Falmouth. I get some sandwiches for the journey from a shop in the town and make my way past the quays and docks narrowly avoiding being stabbed in the eye by an elderly lady struggling with a wayward umbrella. It's a relief as the number of people about gets less and less and I head up to Pendennis Head. This would be a fantastic viewpoint on a clear day, but not today. It is still raining and the wind up here is blowing sharp arrows of water towards me at an almost horizontal degree. I'm so glad I have a decent raincoat. The path follows the road down past the beaches at Gyllyngvase and Swanpool before leaving the built up environment. I am still benefiting from the boost to my creativity that living in Burnham has provided, and as well as the ongoing artistic project based on the DRI, I am also

writing more and more songs. When I pick up my guitar and
intuitively begin playing a chord progression or fingerpicking patten,
then melodies begin to form in my head. This in turn begins to
suggest what the song is about. I usually record the ideas on my
phone, because they will surely be gone and forgotten next time I
have the instrument in hand. I can then begin the process of
constructing a song. When the torrential downpour begins to ease, I
am able to play something on my phone that I have been working on
and start to think about the lyrics.
I have been conscious of the way I can often be dissatisfied and wish
I had been to such and such a place, or done such and such a thing. I
know it is good to have aims and goals but if that is at the expense of
losing some of the joy of what life is giving now, then everything I do
or achieve will never give any contentment. It's good to be able to
write these thoughts down in a song, communicate the ideas to other
people. Much harder to put them into practice in my own life

Wish I'd walked along the Great Wall, and I
Wish I'd been able to risk a fall, oh I
Wish I'd loved as love is now, but I
Still wouldn't change, anything, anyhow
Oooh, ooh, with each new day.... I'm not wishing my life away.

Wish I'd learned a foreign tongue, and I
Wish I'd finished all the things I begun, yes I
Wish I'd never had that awful row, but I
Still wouldn't change, anything, anyhow
Oooh, ooh, with each new day.... I'm not wishing my life away.

Wish I'd gazed on the Taj Mahal, and I
Wish I'd swam in the Bay of Bengal, cos I
Wish I'd given all I can give now, but I
Still wouldn't change, anything, anyhow
Oooh, ooh, with each new day.... I'm not wishing my life away.

Wish I had all the time to spare, and I
Wish I still had a full head of hair. Cos I
Wish I'd known, all that I know now, but I
Still wouldn't change, anything, anyhow
Oooh, ooh, with each new day.... I'm not wishing my life away.

Wish I'd seen the northern lights, and I
Wish I was able to put the world to rights, oh I
Wish that I had not broken a vow, but I
Still wouldn't change, anything, anyhow
Oooh, ooh, with each new day.... I'm not wishing my life away.

The rain has stoped altogether as I follow the inlet of the Helford River to my rendezvous point. Again I'm missing out the ferry crossing and I will begin next time on the other side. It's still only March and I am already over 90 miles of wonderful coastal walking away from the Welcome to Cornwall sign. As the days get longer and warmer I'm sure I am going to really enjoy making my way around this beautiful peninsula.

May 2015
Day 24

Back in Cornwall and we have booked an overnight stay in Helston so I can do 2 days walking. I begin today's stage in the little secluded and seemingly deserted village of Helford, and then along a peaceful river side through glorious bluebell woods. I was not able to cross the little creek by the stepping stones, they were still covered by a high tide. So I followed the pathway around because there was also no sign of a ferry which is mentioned in some of the guide books. It is a few extra miles but it's the start of the day and even though we have driven a long way and then down narrow and poorly signposted country lanes to get here, I'm still full of energy and eager anticipation for the day ahead. Today I passed the the half way mark of the South West Coast Path on Porthallow beach. Not realising I was at that point, I walked passed the official marker plaque without seeing it was there and I carried on to my meet up place at Coverack beach. In one way it is a shame I missed it. It is a point marked out in the landscape and is one of the signifiers that can give a journey significance. It is odd that due the terrible weather conditions when I began this walk, I also missed the plaque which marks the start (or end depending on which way you travel,) of the coast path in Dorset. For me the signifiers are important, like the crossing of a border where the line on a map is realised by a mark in the world. In another way, it is not really something to mind at all, it is just a metal plaque on a beach and the journey continues whether I acknowledge seeing it or not. Nevertheless when I get to Minehead I will make extra effort to stop by the marker, have photo taken and in some way recognise the moment.

Since I was last in Cornwall, the infirmary work has had its first public exhibition. For a week at the Engine Room in Bridgwater, I installed the video triptych. Paintings and drawings complementing and informing the work were also on display. I even had to give a presentation about the work which was both daunting and rewarding. It is good to see it coming together in an exhibition space, and a real incentive to carry on and take the project forward to its next stage.

May 2015
Day 25

Staying last night in Helston means we have no long drive to the the far end of the world before beginning the day's hike. My intention is to make the most of it and walk about 18 miles as far as Mullion Cove. As an added bonus it is a glorious spring day, with a gentle warmth and clear visibility to the horizon. A perfect day for coastal walking. The scenery today does not disappoint as I make my way around The Lizard Peninsula, worthy of its status as an area of outstanding natural beauty. My journey has taken me further and further to the west, but also further and further south. And now I have reached the most southerly point of mainland Britain. I get a real sense of scale, I am a small speck on a small island, looking out into a vast ocean. Because of my familiarity with atlases and maps I know if I could go due south, there would be no more land until the northern Spanish coast, west, nothing until the edge of Newfoundland across the Atlantic.

I am on the fringe of what I know and I think of those old maps that could only show the known explored world because beyond "here be dragons" The sea is a hostile territory. I have swam in it when it is so cold it makes the skin lose any form of sensation, but also when it is as warm as a relaxing bath. I have been on boats when it is as calm as a millpond and also been thrown from side to side when it's been a raging storm. It is not the solid and putatively safe "terra firma" that lies under my feet on this cliff edge now. It is an alien world, the boundary, the "this far and no farther" existing as both a tangible and metaphorical edge. A barrier to, and yet promise of the possibility of something more

CHAPTER 4

NORTH CORNWALL

June 2015
Day 26

I park the car at the little harbour in Mullion Cove and Rob and I get on our boots, load up our rucksacks and prepare for the day's hiking ahead. This is the far west of Cornwall but we have only had to drive from our caravan in Devon so the day is still young. The slight breeze coming from the sea does little to combat the warmth of this June day and I have made sure I have plenty of fluids packed ready for the journey. We agree with Sharon on our rendezvous and make our way up the rocky headland and look back over the beautiful and rugged clash of land and sea that heads back south towards the Lizard. I'm glad to be walking another couple of sections with Rob and I am sure he will relish this magnificent scenery as much as I do. I also hope he has prepared for this as the route will include some ascents and descents which can be quite taxing especially in the midsummer heat. It is a different experience walking with company, the pleasure in seeing a kestrel hovering above, is shared and discussed. The awesome power of the sea crashing against the rocks is seen with renewed appreciation because someone else is sharing the moment. We pass by ruined engine houses and chimneys, the iconic symbols of a once thriving mining industry and find ourselves talking about the shape of a Cornish pasty. Held by the miners on the uneaten crust, so arsenic on the hands was not also consumed with the meat and veg on one side and sweet fruit on the other.

We have walked about 10 miles and are slowly climbing a quite steep section of path. Unfortunately Rob has made the classic mistake and not kept himself sufficiently hydrated for the difficult and hot climb. He begins to feel unwell, breaking out into a cold sweat and he says "he feels like his legs are turning to jelly". Luckily with a sit down, short rest and a good gulp or two of reviving water, he begins to feel a bit better. This is a good job because there's no way I could carry him, and unknown to him we still have over 5 miles to go.

June 2015
Day 27

Where has the lovely June sunshine of yesterday gone? Rob and I are sat in a seafront shelter in Penzance grateful for finding a respite from the rain to eat our lunch. The shape of the fairytale castle on St Michaels Mount slips in and out of sight as swirling mists and rain play peekaboo with my expectation of a good view. The rain has emptied the wide promenade and the the only people about are an older couple also taking shelter from the weather with us. We talk to them about the rain, the constant subject of an English conversation, and then ask "where are you from?" I think about this later, why did I want to know where they lived? It's not just inquisitiveness but part of the human need to make a connection. There is a deep desire within us to be known, these pleasantries of conversation part of a search for someway to connect. Perhaps they live here in Cornwall or maybe they are on holiday and come from somewhere familiar to me, and it's as though if we can find a place where things overlap then that connection can be made. This is a different experience to making lasting relationships, the brief and transitory nature of the exchange is well understood with no expectation of any depth. It is just part of the acknowledgement that to be, I need to know and be known. A connection was made, they came from Newton Abbot, a town in Devon very familiar to me due to family and holiday connections. It is a small world!

The sun begins to break through as we walk up through Newlyn and Mousehole, and I get the view I wanted, back across to the Mount in the bay. It is good to leave the town behind and be back on a coastal path. The sun has very quickly dried the ground and we make our way to Larmorna Cove enjoying the warmth and fresh clean air.

September 2015
Day 28

Today I walked past the busy tourist location of Lands End. I didn't dwell or mingle with the crowds at the photo opportunity signpost, but carried on walking by, taking in the significance of the moment. We had avoided travelling to Cornwall in August, school holidays and an abundance of tourists would have made the roads impassable and accommodation prohibitively priced. I was therefore surprised by the number of people still about on an overcast September day but not surprised by the way everyone seemed to be experiencing the occasion through the lens of a mobile phone.

With every stage of the journey I have carried my phone with me. Necessary for its primary function of contacting Sharon, if my estimates of arrival times at a rendezvous point need last minute adjustments. But very frustrating if no phone signal is available. Useful too, as I didn't need the extra weight of carrying a separate camera, the quality of images from the phone perfectly acceptable for my needs. But the cleverest thing my phone was able to do utilised its built in GPS tracking facility. This doesn't rely on a phone signal but courtesy of the United States military, a series of satellites orbiting the earth at over 12000 miles above me can pinpoint the exact location of my phone to a few metres. As I have already stated, navigating the coast path is not difficult and being old fashioned I like to use my ever familiar ordinance survey map. The GPS however, has enabled me to track my route on my computer when I am back at home, the data being sent automatically by email and showing up on google maps on my screen, a technologically drawn line on a contemporary rendition of a map.

The advances of this technology and our reliance on it seemed to have happened almost imperceptibly. 30 years ago a small hand held communication device, capable of pinpointing its location anywhere on the surface of a planet was purely the stuff of Star Trek. I had not heard of the internet and to see someone whilst talking to them, meant you needed to be in the same room. Yet I cannot remember how or when these changes happened, the constant drip feed of each new advance making me a little like the frog in water, gradually getting warmer and not realising I'm about to be boiled alive.

September 2015
Day 29

I have walked around the headland of Cape Cornwall. My destination is now always to the North and to the East The ground underfoot has become at times quite boggy and at other times stoney and strewn with boulders, uneven and difficult to walk on. Every step has to be carefully considered and my pace slows accordingly. This seems harder walking than some of the steep climbs and descents that the path has to offer, although this stretch of coast is not lacking in those either. This is Poldark country and I even pass carpenters working on an old engine housing. On inquiring I am told they are preparing

some of the external locations for filming the next BBC series.
I do love these sunny September days, perfect for walking. It is warm
but not blisteringly hot, the air is clear, rendering the colours of sea,
land and sky, vivid in detail. As so often on the coast path, the
further away from settlements of human habitation I get, the
presence of local users of the path, out for an afternoon stroll or a
daily walk with their dogs, become less frequent and at times today I
have been in splendid isolation. When there is no one around, this
stretch of coast feels like the edge of the known world.
I am acutely aware of the process of marking out a boundary like the
ancient custom of "beating the bounds" marked the parish boundary.
For me, this is in someway a deeply personal psychological process as
well as a physical process. There is a connection between my notions
of self, my relationships with friends and family, my place in the
world and how I define and mark it and with me being here on this
long journey. There are times during the long walk home when that
realisation seems more present, and here at the far reach of mainland
Britain I get an inkling of some of the multiple layers of meaning I
take from this experience.

October 2015
Day 30

It's the end of October and the days are getting shorter. We have
travelled to Cornwall again with Helen and will do 3 days on the
coast path before finishing until next Spring. It is a long drive all the
way to Zennor but I know my walk is now taking me closer and
closer to home with each mile covered. Every trip away will start not
quite as far away as the one before. Helen and I set of from the car
park and walk the half mile or so up the path back to the coast. As
the sea comes into view we are both struck by the sheer magnificence
of the North Cornish coast, it's fantastic to be back here and walking
again, I'm really looking forward to sharing the experience with my
friend, she had been particularly looking forward to Cornwall and the
terrain does not disappoint.

We hug the coastline, dropping down into valleys and back up to top. Often the path is narrow and we walk single file, the ever present sea crashing against seemingly immutable and immoveable jagged walls of rock. We eat a lunch of sandwiches and crisps, my standard fair when walking, which provides energy enough for the journey. A gastronomic treat not necessary when the vista is this good. Ahead lies St Ives and as we get nearer I know Helen will want to stop and have a cup of tea. I usually walk straight through each town or village eager to be back to the solitude of the lonely path but it will be very pleasant to stop and enjoy a short break. We find a small cafe right on Porthmear beach and sit and watch the rubber clad surfers waiting for the next great wave. Refreshed we keep going along St Ives waterfront, around the island, the harbour and Porthminster beach. As we walk through the trees above Carbis Bay, Helen tells me about coming here as a child. So many people have holiday memories of Cornwall, the feel good factor of sun, sea and sand is deep in the national consciousness.

October 2015
Day 31

Only me walking today. We stayed last night in the Travelodge in Hayle and didn't have a good night. A collapsing bed, an incompetent night manager and poor Helen left traumatised. Sharon and Helen will spend a more leisurely day together giving her time to recover and I will cover a much longer route on my own. I'm dropped back at St Uny's church at Lelant and begin the hike around the Hayle estuary and out onto the long sandy stretch of Hayle Towans Beach. It's cloudy and overcast so except for the occasional wind surfer, the beach is empty and I have a three mile trek until I rejoin the path with only sand underfoot and thoughts in my head. Earlier in the month we had visited Derby and I took another walk around the perimeter of the Derbyshire Royal Infirmary. The process of demolition is now well underway. Internal walls of former wards now exposed to the elements, incongruous colours of yellow and purple revealed like an open wound. The adjoining newer building is still open as a community hospital and as I'm staring at the increasing piles of rubble and bricks, a worker from there walks by and stands to look with me. He tells me he is a painter and decorator and has worked for the hospital in that role his whole working life. " I can remember painting those walls" he tells me, "I never thought I would outlive this place" he mournfully adds. His melancholy seems to sum up the experience. The sense of loss is more than just my personal reaction to the demise of the hospital. It is also part of a shared loss for all those who have had a relationship this with institution at the heart of the city for over 100 years, relationships that encompass the whole range of human emotion. It is that connection, my personal history as it intersects with a larger cultural history that this project is trying to articulate. Meeting the painter and sharing that brief moment was the work in microcosm, and I felt a new incentive to continue making work and begin to draw this project to it's conclusion.

October 2015
Day 32

It is my last day walking on the coast path this year. I have managed to have 15 separate days of walking and covered around 195 miles since I recommenced walking at Portwrinkle in the Spring. Part of me would have liked to have taken a 2 week break and covered the distance, walking every day. Part of me is more realistic, and questions if I would be fit enough to undertake that much of trek all in one long go. Spreading the journey over 8 months has allowed the time to let ideas and thought processes develop and mature, to realise some of the abstract concepts in a concrete way, see how they work as for example in a painting or a song. After each walk, I know that the next time I am alone with my thoughts on a deserted stretch of coast, I can mentally hone and polish the idea and take it to a further expression.
Helen and I are fortunate with good weather and we enjoy the rugged landscape full of the remnants of the former mining industry including the bat friendly covers over long deserted mine shafts. When we descend to the beach at Perranporth we find a town still in full holiday mode. The October sun is shining with a generous

warmth, the sands are crowded, the car park is full and cars are queuing. We both have no phone signal to contact Sharon so we walk away from the beach and hope to see her before she gets stuck in the stationary queue waiting to park. We find somewhere to get a cup of tea and sit outside, relish the autumnal rays of sunshine and wait for our lift to arrive.

March 2016
Day 33

Sharon and I find a nice little cafe in Perranporth and enjoy an excellent English breakfast, and I'm all ready to start walking the coast path again. It has been a long winter's hiatus of nearly 5 months, but I have at least done a little hiking in the Quantocks so it shouldn't be to much of a shock to the system. The short days and dark evenings have also been quite a productive time for making art. Continuing with the form of triptych, I have begun making work on canvas. The central section, a painting of an old fashioned nurse in black and white, juxtaposed with photos of empty wards as the side panels. So many things filter into making work and as I'm painting I'm aware of some of the references. These include a photo of my mother as a nurse in the 1950s, Richard Prince's series of nurse paintings which he based on the covers of cheap novels, photos I have taken in the now empty Bridgwater Infirmary and so much more. Nothing we make as artists stands in isolation, everything is built on and influenced by something else.

Since I was last on the coast path, we have moved from our flat on the sea front in Burnham and are now living in larger place in the centre of town. We no longer have the daily reminder of the changing tides and the view out to horizon. The sound of the sea gently lapping against the shore can no more send us into restful sleep. I am grateful for the time we had and know that living in such a wonderful location was in some way a part of me making this journey. We now live in a much more spacious apartment and can still see the sea from the front window but the panoramic view is now somebody else's to enjoy. Everything is for a season.

I make my way over the sand dunes and onto the long expanse of Perran Beach and although the sun is shining, this early in the year the sands are almost empty. This is a nice way to start back on the journey, fairly level walking with magnificent blue sea and golden sands. The route rounds Crantock beach and along the estuary of the River Gannel before crossing some stepping stones and into Newquay. I find I am walking through a residential area and then past a derelict hotel before reaching the esplanade and Fistral Beach. It seems every parking space on the road is occupied by camper vans, discharging barefooted youngsters in wetsuits down to the famous surf.

March 2016
Day 34

We stayed last night in Newquay and only have a short drive to start today's walk. I want to make the most of staying locally again tonight, so plan to walk about 17 miles today to Harlyn Bay where there is a pub just off the beach in which I will meet Sharon. It's a beautiful spring day and the path going out of the town is alongside a road with the dubious name of Lusty Glaze Road. Some of the expensive looking apartments here probably have views even better than the one we used to have in Burnham. It is as I get further away from people I can really begin to let my mind wander, and for some reason I am thinking about when I was first studying fine art. It wasn't until I was in my 30s that I went to college to pursue my long time interest in art and I remembered a college trip to see the Sensation Exhibition at the Royal Academy. I could talk about how this was is many ways a seminal exhibition for me, helping me to question the idea of what art actually was, but today it was one specific work exhibited in this show which I find occupies my thoughts. "Dead Dad" is a hyperreal sculpture by Ron Mueck. The artist has an incredible attention to detail and by casting with silicone and acrylic creates an exact replica of a naked dead body except in one detail, it is only 3/4 actual size. When I first encountered this at the exhibition, it didn't in any way shock me. And why should it? When I was nursing I had seen many dead bodies and was therefore more impressed with the artist's attention to detail rather than unsettled by the subject. It was for me the scale which gave the work a powerful emotional charge, human frailty diminished by death. It is that emotional response to Mueck's sculpture which I am very conscious of now as I'm walking. I am also very aware that the reason I am revisiting this memory is that I am trying to make sense of what is happening to my own father as he slips further and further away from us, his vascular dementia increasingly changing who he is. Rather than a gradual loss of cognitive function, my dad's condition has been characterised by sudden jump steps down. At what stage do I choose to say farewell? Is there a point where I decide, I'm going to say goodbye now Dad as tomorrow you may not know who I am. Of course not, I hold on to the relationship and weather the changes, because with every loss of the father I have known my whole life, there still remains my dad. Changed, different but still and always my dad. Will there come a point when I look back and think I wish I had said those things then, because now is too late, I don't know the answer to that and must just accept the inevitable progress of natures cruel and pernicious plan.

March 2016
Day 35

Overcast and a little cold today, but it's not raining and I will soon get warm once I'm on my way. I will be walking 15 miles to Port Quinn before driving home. Padstow is about half way and there is another ferry journey which will take me over the River Camel. Even when the weather is a little disappointing, the scenery is still breathtaking and the lack of sun means far fewer people out and about. The journey continues ever northward and eastward, heading closer and closer to home and I realise I'm getting used to this regular exercise, which must be helping to keep me fit. When, and if I do manage to complete my walk all the way to Burnham this year, I will then need to plan another journey and keep up the momentum. And today I find I am making a steady even pace, the terrain not too challenging. The air is very clear and although not sunny I can see a long way ahead. I realise that the headland in the far distance is Hartland Point in Devon. It is one of those wow moments, I'm not far from the next border, and my feet placed on the earth connect with the firmly fixed map located in my mind.

I don't get fed up of this close proximity to the sea and I have to regularly stop, not just to have the occasional rest but because I need to just look and soak up the sheer awesome scale of the view. I also need to stop to make notes as I am walking I am also working on lyrics to a new song and if I don't jot them down on my phone I will have forgotten most of them by the time today's walk is over. I have been working on this song for a while, but it's here at the coast when it begins to make sense to me

She walks through fire, and dances in the rain
She don't get wet and her feet don't feel the pain
She sails up high, across a clear blue sky
With broken wings, she still can fly, away

She takes a breath of Spring and feels alive
Watches the ship come in on the morning tide
She sings redemption songs to me
A voice that carries over land and sea, so free

She listens for the whisper on the wind
One journey ends, another will begin
She tells me tales of hopes and fears
Her story weaves across the years

Hiding every scar, never near but never far
God knows who you are, who you are

April 2016
Day 36

Back in Cornwall for 2 days walking. Once we have left the main road on our drive down, it is a tiny narrow Cornish lane that take us down the hill and back to Port Quinn. The first glimpse of the blue water reminds me of holidays spent with Andy and Shirley. So often disappointed by cold, damp mists rolling in from the sea we would drive from the North coast to the South coast or vice versa in search of the elusive summer sunshine. Nowhere in Cornwall is far from the sea and often when one coastline was dull, overcast and miserable a few miles drive to the other would give a glorious day on the beach.

It is a sunny and clear day and in the blue haze of the distance I can see as far as Lundy Island. I pass through the little town of Port Issac, made famous by the tv series "Doc Martin" and like a true tourist I find myself location spotting. I walk right by the house featured in the programe without even noticing it, and only realise where it was when I'm long passed and looking back down into the town from the path on the other side.
The guide books I have read, describe this part of the coast path as "strenuous" and "challenging". This is an accurate description. I lose count of how many times I descend into a deep valley and have then to slowly climb up the other side. But the views are compensation for the hard physical strain and I feel as if I will have really earned a few ciders tonight.

April 2016
Day 37

Putting on my boots in the car park by the parish church in Tintagel, I can see the route ahead as it passes the ruined 13th century castle. That will be a visit for another day as I'm keen to continue my way around this dramatic Cornish coastline. The very name Tintagel evokes a sense of a mystical past, shrouded by the mists of time and linked to the mythical figure of King Arthur. The nearly 800 year old ruins on the headland actually date from one hundred years after Geoffrey of Monmouth wrote his fabled history of the kings of Britain which tell of Arthur's birth here. So little is recorded of the immediate post Roman period in the history of the British Isles, the era known as the dark ages, that myth and imagination tell as much as the interpretation of evidence. Some places though, seem to retain echoes that stretch way back. The connections to the past, whether because of stories I have previously read and seen or because of something present here, in the now, seem almost tangible.

Walking away from the ruins and with the imposing building of the Camelot Castle Hotel also behind me, it is at first an easy amble along a spectacular cliff top path. So much of this area is familiar, from visits or as in the case of the hotel as a location for the film "The Witches", that I cant help but to reminisce about a day spent on the beach at Bossiney with Michael and Karen. Michael had brought his small inflatable dingy and our eldest son Christopher, who was only about 5 years old at the time, and Karen were rowing and having fun, out in the shallow surf. A larger than expected wave upturned the little boat throwing Chris out and under the water. I can remember the instant panic, Michael, who at the time didn't have children of his own, seemed only worried about losing his oars, whilst Sharon and I are screaming at him to get Chris. The moment was over in a second, Chris back on his feet in the water with no harm done, but how easily the outcome could have been different. Later after some vigorous walking I come down towards the narrow entrance to Boscastle Harbour. Following the little inlet around the corner to the pretty, picturesque village, I cross the little bridge and remember hearing of the terrible floods here in 2004. It's hard to imagine as I stand looking down at the gentle river below me in this sleepy tourist village, the scale of the devastation as torrents of flood water cascaded down this narrow, and deep valley. I know of course that everything I take for granted can change in an instant, our lives would have been very different if the outcome all those years ago in Bossiney was not as it was. Normal everyday life is only as secure as the thin delicate threads that hold it together. But until something happens and those threads become loose, tragedies like Boscastle only ever happen to other people.

April 2016
Day 38

Place names in Britain are so often a clue to the history of an area.
Wave after wave of migration to these shores, whether Celtic,
Roman, Saxon, Viking or Norman have left evidence of their
settlement in the names we still use today. Cornwall has its'
Trebetherick, Trelissick, and Tregony. It has its' Poldhu, Polzeath
and Polkerris and it has its' Pendennis, Penryn and Penzance, all
from the Celtic Cornish language. I start today's walk in a place called
Crackington Haven, which from its's name, seems as though it
should actually be located somewhere to the North, perhaps on the
coast between Scarborough and Whitby.

 I am again very lucky with the spring weather, it's going to be a
glorious day for walking. There is a nice little cafe next to the beach
and Sharon and I eat sausage sandwiches made from local and
extremely tasty sausages. I am planning to walk over 14 miles today
as we are again staying overnight, and I am thankful for the
sustenance because this whole section of coast path contains some of
the hardest coastal walking there is on the South West path. As we
eat, we can see walkers high on the path in the distance. They look
like small specks, the fluorescent colours of the rucksacks vivid
against the muted browns of the headland. That pathway looks a long
way up! And I know when I have scaled the first one that is in front
of me as I am looking now, there will be plenty more to come. It is
an arduous and difficult walk that eventually takes me to Bude. The
town seems very busy compared to the isolation of a preceding
stretch of coast path. As the way leads down from the grassy green
headland, alongside the Bude Canal and into the town, the sheer
amount of people slowly ambling along and enjoying the sunny
seaside location seem at odds with my purposeful ever onward stride.
I have to admit I actually feel irritated by slow moving people not

seeing me coming and standing aside to let me pass. Sometimes I can be a very ungracious individual and so I chide myself, slow down and go with the flow. Very soon Bude is behind me, and regretting my impatience I carry on in solitude towards my rendezvous with Sharon.

April 2016
Day 39

Sharon drops me at Duckpool Beach and drives back up the narrow lane towards civilisation. Today will be my last section of coast path in Cornwall, and it is with a sense of excitement that I begin the slow ascent from the car park onto the rocky narrow path which seems to be getting narrower and narrower the higher I climb. The path doesn't disappear into nothing and soon I am walking next to the razor wire surrounding the perimeter of the satellite ground station on the top of an isolated cliff. Because of the security and forbidding signs, I expect this is not part of the telecommunications network that can enable me to make an international telephone call, but is more likely to be technology that can be used to listen in to that call if it was deemed I was a threat to national security. What freedoms must be sacrificed to keep us free? I am unable to resist taking a photograph of the "no photography" sign.

As I reach the bottom of a particularly difficult descent, going downhill can take as much effort as going up sometimes, I see two figures slowly making their way to the next summit. When they reach the top, they are silhouetted against the sky, small slowly moving shapes, disappearing out of sight. People I will never know, who have experienced this section of coast at the same time as me and then go on and live an existence completely unknown to me.

The line on the ordnance survey which indicates the county border is difficult to see, just a light grey dot dash like morse code on the page. The contour lines either side of the valley through which the border runs are densely packed, It tells me it is going to be to be a steep descent. Seeing the valley ahead I know on the other side is Devon. Yet when I get to the bottom and cross the little bridge and see the marker posts, the familiar acorn symbol and yellow arrow pointing the way, Cornwall in one direction and Devon the other, I find the conformation reassuring. It is a border I can cross, no customs post or passport control, one local administration to another. It makes me think of borders which are harder to cross, borders to protect the haves from the have nots. Borders which have kept people in and those to keep others out. Borders drawn far away on maps to carve up somebody else wealth. Borders which time has eroded and made irrelevant and the borders we think will last forever, but of course will not

CHAPTER 5

NORTH DEVON

June 2016
Day 40

We have another overnight stay booked so I can do 2 days and over 30 miles of coastal walking. The journeys down to the start of each day's walk are getting shorter and shorter as each start point gets nearer and nearer to home. I am hoping after this trip away, I will be close enough to home to do subsequent walks as day trips.

I start today at Hartland Quay, and am now walking in Devon. We are staying in Devon and Cornwall is behind me, consigned to photos and used ordnance survey maps

I'm now following the path on my 14th map and all the detailed inland information hardly looked at, I have the complete map but all I require is just the coastal margin. To follow a map on the page of a guide book is not the same as being able to lay out a whole sheet on the floor and see where I have been in relation to all that surrounds me.

I have been thinking that it is time now to bring the infirmary project to a close. Sometimes decisions about how to articulate my ideas are influenced by practical considerations and I have 3 large, primed unused canvases left, so it seems I need to paint one final triptych. It is the idea of maps that is really exciting me. Perhaps there is a crossover with this walk, maybe it could be the marking out the miles on a 2 dimensional surface that ties in with the final piece of work about the hospital.

I have been researching the site plans that all large hospitals have, the guides on how find your way around what is to some people a frightening and unfamiliar environment. They seem almost like abstract paintings and yet somehow manage to represent a real place in a graphic format. It is the plans of both the Royal Infirmary and also Kingsway psychiatric hospital that will form the basis of 2 of the paintings for the triptych. As a student general nurse I spent a 9 week allocation working in the acute admissions ward at Kingsway, it was in many ways an experience which has affected who I am as much as the time I spent working on general wards.

I am walking through glorious woodland scenery. The ground underfoot is quite slippery due to recent rain, so I have to watch each step but the woods are a tranquil and peaceful place. The coast path does not go through the little village of Clovelly but follows a route from which you can look down to the famous harbour. I could, for a small fee descend and join the many tourists around, and see the little, traffic free cobbled high street but decide to keep to the official path. I later find out that the entrance fee is payable at the car park and as I walked in along the coast path I would have avoided having to pay it but as I was unaware of this, I made the decision not to go into the village. On this journey I will have passed through every town, village and hamlet in the South West peninsular that lie at the edge of the land. All except for the privately owned Clovelly.

June 2016
Day 41

Yesterdays walk took it's toll on my knee, and caused me more discomfort than it has ever done before. Even after taking a dose of

Voltorol, it was uncomfortable overnight. Sharon drops me at the little car park in Bucks Mills so I can retrace my steps along the country lane, with the little stream running alongside to reach the marker post with it's instantly recognisable little acorn that points away up the side of the valley. As soon as I start to walk I get a sharp stab in the side of the knee, oh no I have over 15 miles to go before I reach our meet up point in Bideford. Gritting my teeth I stride of and luckily It settles into a dull ache. Keep taking the tablets!

This beautiful section of coast is deserted, I walk through dappled summer woods and down to empty beaches of large stones and bleached driftwood. Sitting on a washed up half tree trunk I look out to sea. This is now the Bristol Channel, and I wonder at what point along this stretch of coast the blue turns to the brown and grey water I am used to at home.

Westward Ho! The only town with an exclamation mark in it's name gives me a chance to buy an ice-cream and to sit down and nurse my slowly swelling knee joint. Next my route will follow the long sandy beach and round alongside the estuary of the Rivers Taw and Torridge and to Appledore before following the Torridge into Bideford. I am briefly tempted follow the road out of Westward Ho!, cut out the long loop and reach my destination having saved a few painful miles. I know I would feel I had cheated and not completed the whole route of South West Coast Path so decide against and walk out beside the golf course with the water as always, to my left side. Fortunately the terrain is very flat and my knee doesn't complain too much.

The frailty of the flesh, surely we are more than just this fragile skin and bone.

All that's lost, and all that's found
All you hear, without a sound
Every truth, and every lie
The shallow breath, before you die
All you hide, all you've been shown
Everything, that can be known
So much more than skin and bone

The faces, only once seen
All the places, that you've ever been
All the friends and the hands you hold
All the stories you've been told
All the times when you're alone
And you wish you were going home
So much more than skin and bone

All the colours, the rainbow hue
All you've done and are yet to do
All the words you wish you'd not said
And all the thoughts inside your head
When you reap the seeds you've sewn
Can you crush the blood from a stone
So much more than skin and bone

The distance across to Saunton Sands seems little more than a short hop, but the coast path follows the river and there is about 20 miles to cover before I reach that tantalisingly close section. I meet up with Sharon in Bideford's Wetherspoon's for a nice cold drink before the drive home. This will make a good place to start the next section in a week or so's time as I can have a filling breakfast to give me energy for the walk ahead.

June 2016
Day 42

Back in Bideford for a days walk. We are close enough to home now to do this as a day trip, and it will be nice to sleep in my own bed tonight. My knee seems ok, so after my promised sausage and bacon breakfast, I cross the town bridge and join the Tarka Trail, a long distance cycle and walking path which doubles up with the coast path for this next section.

The tide is low and although I'm not familiar with this route around the estuaries of the rivers Taw and Torridge, the stranded sailing boats looking all forlorn and the flat riverside views remind me of the landscape of home.

This is the coast path demonstrating another of its many variations. Coastal walking is not all stunning clifftop views and golden beaches but can in fact sometimes be dull and boring. Crossing the road bridge in Barnstaple involves walking along side busy traffic which is no pleasure at all but this is the route I am following, the same path which will eventually lead to my front door.

Leaving the town and heading for Braunton I pass on my left, protected by a formidable fence the military base at Chivenor. I watch as an olive green military Land Rover is permitted under the barrier and disappears into the unknown. I am aware of a personal contradiction. A life in any of the services would not have suited me and I find many aspects of the military ethos to be an anathema to me. Perhaps because I spent my early years growing up in a forces family, living as part of an army community, I have a strange fascination with what goes on behind the barbed wire. Not enough to make me linger and I head to my rendezvous with the unfinished lyrics to a new song waiting to be completed in my head. The voice recognition software on my phone is such an advantage as typing on the tiny keyboard whilst looking where you are going can be quite difficult

Sweet the taste of summer rain, nectar from the sky
Fresh the early morning dew, each new day's sunrise
Felt the sand beneath my feet, walking on the shore
Looked out over the ocean waves, and cannot want for more

Here, you're here with me
So I've got everything, everything I need

Listened to the rising lark, on a cloudless summers day
Watched out for the shooting stars, across the Milky Way
Climbed the hill and seen the view from Glastonbury Tor
Smelt the rose with it's prickly thorn, and cannot want for more

Here, you're here with me
So I've got everything, everything I need

Mercedes cars, new guitars or that fancy diamond ring
I don't suppose I'll ever know, what too much money brings,
But I don't mind, no I don't care, I know that I am sure
You are here , here with me and I cannot want for more

Here, you're here with me
So I've got everything, everything I need

July 2016
Day 43

Walking again with Rob on a stretch of coastline that includes river
estuary, sand dunes, cliff tops, long expanses of sandy beaches and
plenty of summer visitors. It's the middle of the school holidays and
the glorious North Devon resorts are a sea, sun and surf magnet.
Families playing ball games and splashing in the waves just as Rob
and I, with our friends and families, had done on these very same
sandy playgrounds in years gone by.

I have been struggling with how to finish the infirmary project. One
last painting to complete the final triptych. Research has included
looking at old maps of Scutari in Turkey, where Florence Nightingale
set up her hospital during the Crimean war. Making a painting which
juxtaposes contemporary arial views with 19th century maps and
entitling it "Scutari" could have an interesting connection with the
other 2 parts of the triptych. The Kingsway hospital piece is called
"Sanctuary" and the Royal Infirmary work has been titled "Succour".
Yet somehow I am unable to work this research into a final image. I
have looked at so many hospital information maps, satellite images
and faded black and white pictures that it's all becoming a blur.
Nothing seems to be quite right. The answer eventually is obvious.
The triptych will always be unfinished. Not everything ends with a

neat conclusion. Often we move through life, unknowingly starting a new phase before realising the last has ended. My experience of being a nurse was like that, it could have been a lifetimes career but ended up as only a small but influential part of a longer journey. Another stream of existence feeding into the river of life.

July 2016
Day 44

We park in the pub car park at Mortenhoe and I'm eager to be back on rugged coastal path. The long river estuaries and sandy beaches experienced on the last few sections, now give way to North Devon's stunning cliff top scenery with views across the Bristol Channel to Wales.
The sea is still a beautiful blue reflecting the summer sky but I know as I progress further and further east, the channel will narrow, the Welsh coast will get closer and the increasing turbidity of the water will begin to turn the sea to the familiar browny grey that I am used to at home.

  Because I am able to see the 35 miles or so, over towards the Gower Peninsula, it makes me think about my long time interest in mapping. Some artists would like to capture this stunning view in a 2 dimensional representation, a painting or a photograph, but my minds eye can visualise this location as a map or as an aerial image from above. Following on from the last map pieces of the hospital project this could be an interesting way of developing my artistic practice. The walk itself, is in some way is part of what I do as an artist. I need now to consider how I document that, how I visually represent this experience and articulate something of what the journey means to others.

  Ilfracombe is very busy as I walk through. English seaside towns are still popular with summer visitors and although the Victorian facades seem tired and worn, on this warm July day there is still a pleasant holiday ambience. I'm very keen to see Damien Hirst's large bronze statue on the harbourside. I have seen pictures and read about "Verity" but am still surprised when I encounter her enormous scale. She is still visible as I follow the coast path out of the town and up on to the high Devon cliffs.

There is a very brief section of walking alongside the A399 before I reach Combe Martin and this takes me past the road sign for Berrynarbor. I think back to when I was doing my art degree in Exeter. My practice as a student involved working with photographic images, not only from my own family archive but also from found images. I was finding ways to re-present these captured moments in time and exploring how meaning was communicated. Not only from the faded faces staring out from long ago but also from the descriptions written on the backs of the photos. I had an album of photos from the 1920s and 30s which I had bought from a second hand market stall in Newton Abbot. How is it that somebody's once precious memories are lost to those who's lives are recorded and are on sale as nostalgia. A fellow student was looking through the album when he recognised the location. "that's the cottage where I lived in Berrynarbour when I first moved to Devon, in the 1980s" he said. Taking the small black and white image of a happy couple standing outside a little cottage, from the album, we turned it over to see the description "Berrynarbor 1931" What is it that places this image so firmly in the past? The location still looked the same to my colleague 50 years later and the expressions show a familiar self consciousness when posing for the camera, yet this image is very firmly located in a time gone by. The photo has something universal and timeless and yet was also personal and specific. This was fascinating to me and led me into a whole new body of work.

August 2016
Day 45

August is a wonderful time to be walking along the high cliff tops of North Devon where Exmoor meets the sea. The glorious purple heather is in full bloom and covers the steep descent down to the sea like a richly coloured deep pile carpet. I am walking again with Helen, this particular part of the coast being a section she was very keen to do as we will pass Lee Abbey, somewhere that holds fond memories for her.

It is a steep climb from Combe Martin and we eventually reach Great Hangman which is the highest point on the whole of the South West coast path. But where there are high cliff tops, there are also deep valleys and with this challenging walk we are both grateful that it is a slightly overcast day, which provides us with some protection from the August sun.

This month I have had a distraction from making new art, as I have been asked to contribute some work, made quite a few years ago, to an exhibition at the Tropicana in Weston. Following the success of Banksy's Dismaland, the space is continuing to be used over the summer, to exhibit art and it is quite an accolade to be included as part what is happening at this location. Also taking part is an artist whom I was in a group exhibition with, in London a few years ago, an artist who is making quite a name for himself in the contemporary art field. It is interesting to see how other people's careers progress, and of course I'm not jealous, I continue to make my living as a chiropodist. Who needs success as an artist!

Today's walk is a wonderful contrast of scenery, wild open moors and beautiful shady woodland, Helen even poses for a photo, washing her hair under a crystal clear and ice cold waterfall. We reach Lee Abbey and find not only that the cafe is still open, but Sharon is already there enjoying a Devon cream tea, it would be rude not to have a scone, jam and clotted cream as well. I leave the girls to enjoy refreshments and I continue on my own for the last few more miles through the spectacular Vally of the Rocks. Soon I am heading back down to sea level at Lynmouth, leaving the next steep climb for my next walk.

August 2016
Day 46

I went without Sharon today, and drove on my own to Porlock on
the Somerset coast. I had checked the internet and discovered a bus
which runs from Porlock to Lynmouth and decided to park at the
end of the days coastal hike and catch the bus to my start. What a
nice but expensive bus ride. The journey is a tourist trip in an bright
yellow antique 1950s bus. How it managed to tackle Porlock Hill is a
mystery. The road climbs 725 feet in just under 1 mile, and is the
steepest gradient on any A-road in the country. We slowly made our
way along the coast road and I was able to see from the comfort of
my seat, parts of the path I was about to tackle.

   It is a steep walk out of Lynmouth and up Countisbury hill and I am
finding I need to rub in voltorol gel and wear a knee support more
and more often but I was keen to reach the top and make my way to
Foreland point. The headland is the most northerly point in Devon
and also the most distant part of the coast that can be seen from
Burnham on Sea. It is a day of sunshine and showers and I am
hoping it will be clear enough to see all the way back to Burnham but
a low sea mist obscures the distance and I must console myself with
knowing the end of my journey although not actually in sight, is not
that far at all.

   The route leaves the moorland and continues for miles and miles
through empty woodland. I cross the last border and am in my home
county of Somerset. There doesn't seem to be any marker to
acknowledge this last crossing but the line on the map is all the
evidence I need.

   I don't meet another soul as I make my way under a dense
canopy of summer foliage, except for an inquisitive deer, who eyes

me up and down before disappearing into the undergrowth. I really enjoy the solitude, with only thoughts for company. The deteriorating progression of my dad's illness is an ever present concern. He is now in a nursing home, slowly losing more and more of his mobility, and his once big booming voice becoming just a quiet whisper. The disease is robbing him of his grasp on reality but even amidst the confusion, his face lights up when we visit and he still knows who we are

CHAPTER 6

SOMERSET

September 2016
Day 47

After a light snack with Sharon in a little cafe in Porlock, I walk back down the lane which leads onto the coast path. In less than 10 miles, I will reach Minehead, the point where the South West Coast Path, national long distance trail begins or ends, depending which way round you go. For many walkers Minehead is the start of a 630 mile epic journey. For me it will be a point on the route, a significant staging post, a marker to say I have nearly finished my long walk home.

I am already beginning to plan what comes next. Should this be part of an attempt to walk the whole coastline around Britain? Maybe a little too ambitious to consider that, at this stage. But I am still intrigued by borders, the lines on a map that tie into a rich history of our many and varied identities. The Welsh coast looks very close and I consider that it might be interesting to continue past home, up the Bristol channel and over the Severn Bridge to embark on the Welsh Coast Path. The notions of borders, what they are and what they mean, still buzz around my mind. I then realise the obvious route to go. My next journey will be the national trail that works it's way across the border country between England and Wales. The Offa's

Dyke path follows the route of an ancient earthwork, constructed in the in the 8th century as a border between the Saxon Kingdom of Mercia and the Welsh. A time when a border was more than a line on the map, but a physical defence against a very real threat of attack. It is disconcerting how these ideas still percolate down through the ages and influence how we think of those, whom are considered to be "other". That a border can still be an obstacle to sharing what we have with those unlucky enough to be born on the other side.

When the path reaches it's end at Prestayn on the North Wales coast, I could then begin an anticlockwise navigation of the Welsh Coast Path and find myself on an even longer "way home".

I have reached the moorland at the top of the climb from the marshland and shingly beach, and can see clearly across to Wales. It's only me here, apart from a few Exmoor ponies and I am really enjoying the wonderful vista. Yes a long walk home around the edge of Wales would be an exciting, challenging and hopefully rewarding next adventure!

September 2016
Day 48

It feels strange to no longer be on the South West Coast Path. There are still the little acorn symbols on the very new signposts, but this is now the West Somerset Path, part of the England Coast Path and yes the sea water is a familiar brown and grey, even under a bright September sun. The England Coast Path will be a new national trail around England's coast. It is opening bit by bit and the new signage here is part of the recently completed section from Minehead to Brean. The little acorns will now lead me all the way into Burnham. The tide is a long way out and I walk many miles along nearly empty beaches. I am delighted to see an ammonite within the limestone rocks. It is tempting to spend some time looking for these but I have more than 15 miles to cover today before meeting Sharon at a tiny place, way off the main road, called Stolford. When I am back up off the beach, on an easy path next to a recently ploughed field, I get a sight of home in the distance. The tiny pier on Burnham's seafront has had a new lick of white paint and stands out on the distant coastline like a beacon, pinpointing my final destination. Before it, a fews miles further along the path ahead, is another coastal structure, which is visible from miles around, the nuclear power plant at Hinkley Point.

I am not going to discuss the pros and cons of nuclear energy, but Hinkley has recently been the subject of a very controversial decision. The approval having been granted for the construction of a new reactor, to be built by a French company and funded with Chinese capital. Apart from the huge inconvenience to me of a large detour around both the existing power stations and vast empty building site, the coast path having been diverted away from the coast to go around the facility, the wisdom of the whole venture does seem questionable. Perhaps because I look a little dodgy complete with a suspicious ruck sack, perhaps it's because of a heightened state of security given the recent decision, but as my journey takes me past the road down to the main gate, I am stopped by a passing police car and asked why I am there. My natural charm wins them over and together we consult my map. They very kindly show me the best way to continue along the path, and don't even ask to see inside my backpack.

October 2016
Day 49

It is the penultimate stage of the journey. My route will take me along the River Parrett Trail into Bridgwater before beginning the return along the opposite bank. For most of today's walk I can look across the river to where I will be walking on the final leg back to Burnham. After so much spectacular scenery experienced during my long walk home, the level ground, muddy river and marshy estuary of these last 2 sections, could be considered somewhat uninspiring. Nevertheless I love Somerset, it is a beautiful and varied county. There are the Quantock hills with views across to Wales or down to Devon. There are the Levels, a magical marsh with the Isle of Avalon rising out of the morning mists. The Mendip Hills with the fracture of Cheddar Gorge cutting through the limestone pasture. But the Somerset coast is considered by some as a poor comparison to the rest of the South West. The Bristol Channel and mouth of the River Seven, are not without their own special charm. It has the second highest tidal range in the world which makes for a very different coastal experience than the high rugged cliffs of Cornwall, the extensive mud flats a unique habitat and home for many species of wintering bird life. And at least there is a coast and that is a definite bonus. When I reach Steart, I sit and eat a sandwich in the birdwatcher's hideout, and look across the estuary towards Burnham. It is only a few miles away as the crow flies but well over 20 to walk. I decide to consult my Ordnance Survey map and visualise the distances in my familiar way. Then I realise I have forgotten to bring it with me. Even though I have previously walked this path, know the route, so can't get lost, it seems strange not to have my usual companion my pocket.

These closing stages of the walk are a time to reflect on the journey as a whole, and acknowledge it has been a productive time in terms of my creativity. Visual art and songwriting have had a space to grow and develop. It seems somewhat fitting that the song I am working on now, as I'm nearing the end of a coastal walk, is called " Down by the Sea".

Sit me down by the sea
Let the waves wash over me
Between, the moment and a dream
Sit me down,
Sit me down, sit me down by the sea

Take me down to the rivers side
However hard that I have tried
And all the tears I cried
Take me down,
Take me down to the river, the rivers side

Lead me through this desert land
Never let go, of my hand

Though I am scorched by the wind and sand
Lead me through,
Lead me through, lead me through this desert land

Walk me by trees blazing gold
As the summer sky grows old
Have no fear of the coming cold
Walk me by
Walk me by, walk me by trees blazing gold

Lift me up to the mountain high
And when the sun, she shines too bright
Under eagles wings to hide
Lift me up,
Lift me up, lift me up to the mountain high

Sit me down by the sea
Let the waves wash over me
Between, the moment and a dream
Sit me down,
Sit me down, sit me down by the sea

Now is the time to think about the places I have been, the views I
have seen and perhaps time to consider what the walk has meant. I
have made a few notes as I have walked, taken a few photographs
and logged each day on a Facebook page. So I am going to go back
to the beginning in my mind and try to find ways of articulating the
experience, and that is how writing this document was begun.

November 2016
Day 50

The last day of the long walk home! I would have liked to complete
this last 12 mile section along the River Parrett and back to Burnham
with the two companions who have shared some of the walking with
me. Rob is unfortunately unable to make it so it's just Helen and I

who set off from the car park of the Admiral's Table pub at Dunball Warf, after being dropped off by Sharon. This is quite fitting as it was Helen and I who waved goodbye to our lift, Sharon, in the rainy car park at South Haven Point nearly 3 years previously.

The last few days have been very difficult and I'm thankful to be out walking, able to take the therapy that only a good long walk seems to be able to provide as well as have the opportunity to talk with my friend Helen. Last year, friends of many years, suffered the enormous and devastating loss of a son. A troubled young man, let down by a seemingly uncaring system, ended his own life. This isn't the place to discuss the details other than to say that we have been present with our friends as they have had to go through the long awaited and arduous process of the inquest. And now as I'm walking, I find that somehow being out, away from the everyday minutiae of life, helps to lift the emotional cloud that hovers over me. If I am feeling like this, God only knows the depths of despair and anguish felt by our friends. An inquest can easily become just an investigation of circumstances and details, the person whom the inquest is about frequently lost in the process. At the start of giving his evidence, our friend produced a photograph of his son and showed it to the court, immediately grounding everyone as to the why we were all there. This had been a real, living, breathing, loving and much loved person, not just an abstraction to be discussed. It was a very poignant and powerful moment.

Helen and I reach the mouth of the River Brue as it trickles gently at low tide into the estuary of the River Parrett. Burnham beach is a few hundred feet away across an impossible last border of deep impenetrable mud. We must walk down the river and cross at the sluice gate in Highbridge. This is the last couple of miles. I expected to feel more excited, more of a sense of accomplishment that I was very nearly home, yet the familiar footpath, complete with the dog walkers and afternoon strollers, is a bit of an anticlimax. It is as we reach the boat yard and start down the long esplanade that the reality of the situation begins to dawn. This is Burnham on Sea, my home town, there is the supermarket recently closed and turned into a bargain store, here is the hovercraft station, the saviour of many a foolish tourist stuck out in the mud. These are the last few yards along my seafront, in my town, the last steps of my long walk home. Sharon has come to meet us, as we reach the pier and takes the final photos. All that remains is to walk all together up to the front door. I am home.

CONCLUSION

"End? No, the journey doesn't end here. Death is just another path, one that we all must take. The grey rain-curtain of this world rolls back, and all turns to silver glass, and then you see it."
J.R.R. Tolkien, The Return of the King

I have walked over 686 miles and followed the route on 15 different ordnance survey explorer maps. There have been 50 separate days of walking over a 2 and a half year period and the journey has ended. But I think I am beginning to understand what Gandalf is talking about in the quote from Tolkien, "the journey doesn't end here"

My practice as an artist is concerned with the places an individual journey meets with the universal stories we all know. The derelict hospital was the perfect metaphor, my history as a nurse in Derby and the institution in that city, central to so many peoples encounters with birth, life and death. A place where all life's tragedies and joys were played out. Walking is also a perfect metaphor. Whether it was when I walked the boundary of the hospital grounds, peering in through the fencing to see the once public place made private and hidden or now as I have walked the boundary of the South West Peninsular and this time looked out to an open expanse of blue. In those journeys, I was trying to make connections with my experiences and finding ways to make sense of those experiences.

Over the course of my time navigating the fringes of one world, my father's health gradually declined, the edges of his world shrinking into an ever smaller horizon. I think my time alone with my thoughts has helped me to come to terms with and understand what was happening and how I have felt about it. Two days after I reached the end of the walk, my father also began the last stage of the journey he was on.

On a Monday evening in November, staff at the Nursing home, my dad's home for the previous 5 months, called the doctor as they were concerned about Dad's lack of responsiveness. The GP thought Dad, had maybe suffered a stroke and called the ambulance. The NHS, although, struggling with insufficient resources and very high demand, responded with a level of care unequaled anywhere in the world. Sepsis was suspected and ruled out, and after many tests it was realised that his condition was the inevitable progression of the vascular dementia, his body was shutting down. Consulting with us as a family at every turn, it was decided that Dad would be more comfortable, less stressed and best in his own environment for what is called "end of life care". So that is what happened. An ambulance took Dad back to his own room in the home and we all gathered round with the support of the staff at the home and the district nursing team, to be with him, in those last moments.

How do I begin to make sense of this experience, being with my father as he crossed the last border, journeyed through the space between life and death. In some ways my time as a nurse has prepared me for this, I have been the sympathetic health care professional, witnessing other people's encounter with this, one of the most profound of life's moments. And yet I can no longer end my shift, go home and leave the grief behind. I think that maybe it is this transition, this inevitable path we walk that has been the truth I have been trying to understand, the universal reality of existence that has propelled me to try to articulate through art, through music, what is common to us all.

Words form in my mind, not a song but the just need to express something of what is happening.

I watch as you shrink into the hollow of your face
Diminished except for the love and grace
With every breath your fragile frame
fades away and is no longer the same
A grip so strong so my hand is crushed
Time is still but time is rushed
Say goodbye, can't say goodbye

And so Dad made that last journey, we held his hand, my mum
telling him he was precious, was loved. His final moment, after 3
days of gradually slowing breathing, of a fixed unresponsive
expression, was a smile. Not just the final expulsion of air from the
lungs forming a shape to the lips, but an actual smile and then
silence.

And life carries on, shops open, people go to work and they don't
realise how unreasonable it is when the world has completely
changed. Why would anyone stop their everyday routine, this is the
road we are all walking and none of us know when we will reach our
destination.

The sun rose again today
In its most unreasonable way
As nothing and everything changed
The sun rose again today
So leave me alone
Let me curl up and sleep, let me be on my own
Because
The sun rose again today
In its most unreasonable way
As nothing and everything changed
The sun rose again today

The tide rolled in again today,
In its most unreasonable way
In the difference it remains the same
For the tide rolled in again today
Why does it seem,

the world carries on yet this is just a dream
The tide rolled in again today,
In its most unreasonable way
In the difference it remains the same
For the tide rolled in again today

I watched the sunset today
In its most unreasonable way
And the day light faded to grey
I watched the sunset today

ABOUT THE AUTHOR

Dave Eldergill is an artist, song writer and former nurse living in Somerset

27344461R00049

Printed in Poland
by Amazon Fulfillment
Poland Sp. z o.o., Wrocław